ADAM M. CLARE

THE **UNOFFICIAL**
POKÉMON®
GO!
TRACKER'S GUIDE

PAGE
TWO
BOOKS

Page Two Books
9 West Broadway
Vancouver BC V5Y 1P1
www.pagetwobooks.com

Distributed in Canada by
Publishers Group Canada
300-76 Stafford Street
Toronto ON M6J 2S1

Distributed in the U.S.
and other territories by
Publishers Group West
1700 Fourth Street
Berkeley CA 94710

Cataloguing data available from
Library and Archives Canada
ISBN 978-0-9952665-0-6 (paperback)
ISBN 978-0-9952665-1-3 (ebook)

Editing by Erin Parker
Proofreading by Shirarose Wilensky
Design by Peter Cocking
Cover illustration by Brian Tong
Interior illustrations by Brian Tong
with assistance from Jon Izen
Printed and bound in Canada
by Friesens

16 17 18 19 20   5 4 3 2 1

This book is an unauthorized/ unofficial guide.

CONTENTS

"Traveling—it leaves you speechless,
then turns you into a storyteller."

IBN BATTUTAH, *THE TRAVELS OF IBN BATTUTAH*

INTRODUCTION

The world of games will never be the same. Since its release in the summer of 2016, Pokémon Go has done something that very few games have done: capture our imagination, inspire us to explore outside, and turn strangers into friends. Niantic, the makers of PoGo, released the game at the right time.

The incorporation of augmented reality (AR) into the game has literally made people look at games and their neighborhoods differently.

Although other games have done similar things with augmented reality, none of them has had such an impact around the world in terms of player numbers and appeal. By combining the wow factor of AR with the thrill of catching Pokémon anywhere, Niantic struck gamer gold.

As a game professor and designer, I understand what appeals to players. In the classroom, in the game studio I run, and beyond, I have seen games come and go. Pokémon Go has done something unique by being in the right place at the right time with the right brand.

Around the world, people are placing lures and making new friends. PoGo is changing our culture by bringing more people to social gameplay and by encouraging individuals to take a lead in using the game to engender community.

Everywhere PoGo has been released there are stories about the game improving lives. Because the game gets players walking, countless trainers have gotten healthier by catching Pokémon. Hospitals have used the game to get patients moving. PETA has even hopped on the bandwagon, joining forces with Smiths singer, Morrissey, to develop a mobile game based on PoGo, but with a vegan-friendly slant.

PoGo holds 5 Guinness World Records!

Tourist destinations have caught on that the game encourages travel. Thailand wants additional PokéStops and gyms to attract even more visitors. Their tourism ministry has said that they will even go so far as to create a map and guide specifically for Pokémon Go trainers. In Japan, they are using

More people have downloaded Pokémon Go than Tinder—now this is how you meet people!

TO GET THE GOLD BACKPACKER MEDAL, VISIT TWO THOUSAND POKÉSTOPS!

the game to bring people back into earthquake-damaged areas to promote economic growth. A struggling ice cream parlor in the state of Washington was saved when people flocked to nearby PokéStops. The owner joked, "The Pokémon God came down and shined his light on me!"

All of this because of a game!

Online, too, the reaction to PoGo has been enthusiastic, except when it comes to unsafe and disrespectful actions taken by players, such as walking on subway tracks, leaving a mess at popular PokéStops, or trespassing on private and restricted property. Media reports are mixed, but any trainer knows that the game—played responsibly—is a grand social adventure.

What better way to be social and play the game than by traveling the world! We have selected some of the best, strangest, and coolest locations to play PoGo. Chapter 1 takes you on a tour of our favorite creepy places, from haunted shipwrecks to Area 51 to abandoned mental institutions. Chapter 2 will appeal to trainers with artistic flair who are searching for beautiful concert halls and bizarre statues, musical festivals and literary destinations. Chapter 3 encompasses famous ancient and modern landmarks around the world, like the Egyptian pyramids, the White House, and the Taj Mahal. For urban places, from hectic transit hubs to college campuses, look no further than Chapter 4. Chapter 5 explores natural places, such as volcanoes, waterfalls, prairies, and mountains. In Chapter 6, our focus shifts to dangerous, inappropriate, or otherwise off-limits places we recommend avoiding.

It can be hard to find these places on your own, which is why we assembled the locations in one handy field guide. You can plan your trips around some of these PokéStops or, if you already have a place in mind, the guide can point you towards a gym off the beaten path. Even when your batteries are dead from a day of catching Pokémon, you can open this book and get inspired. We want your trip to remote places that have few electrical hookups to still be filled with Pokémon. Most of the places we've selected have multiple PokéStops. Even if they request to be delisted, there are likely many other stops and gyms nearby.

Even when your batteries are dead from a day of catching Pokémon, you can open this book and get inspired.

Like a true Pokémon Master, you need to be ready to confront any hardships that come your way. Any obstacle in your path is just one more challenge that you'll have to confront. Look to Chapter 7 for tips to make your journey safer and more productive.

May this guide help you on your journey to catch 'em all!

CREEPY PLACES

What's creepy to one person may be fascinating to another. Do you stay clear of abandoned mental institutions and the sites of murders, spooky occurrences, and strange events, or do you seek them out? What might look like an old building or an innocent suburban home can actually harbor something much more sinister. Make sure you bring a trainer you trust when going to these places.

Walter White's House · Albuquerque, New Mexico, USA

There's no doubt that real drug dens are creepy, but they are also quite dangerous. For a safer journey you can swing by a suburban PokéStop. Walter White was the main character in the hit TV show *Breaking Bad*. In the series, White's heartless pursuit to become the best meth cook in the country cost many lives. While at the site, please don't accept any "candy." Many memorable scenes were filmed at this house. Indeed, much of the series was shot in this small New Mexico town. You can do a short *Breaking Bad* tour, if you'd like; after seeing the house, you can head over to battle at the gym A-1 Car Wash. As the actual house is private property, please respect the wishes of the people who live here by not trespassing, throwing pizza on their house, or otherwise being bothersome. Essentially, don't be a creep.

Harry Houdini's Tomb, Machpelah Cemetery · Queens, New York, USA

In New York City, under the crest of the Society of American Magicians, lies Harry Houdini. The tomb of the famous illusionist and stunt performer is a PokéStop. The tomb includes a moving sculpture and bench for resting and reflecting. Some speculated that Houdini's final stunt would be coming back from the dead. Sadly, it's been almost a hundred years since his death and there are no signs that his death was another illusion. There's no word of whether anybody has seen Abra or Kadabra at the tomb.

Area 51, Edwards Air Force Base · Nevada, USA

Since the alleged UFO crash in the Nevada desert, Area 51 has been home to ███████ and conspiracy theories. The heavily secured and secretive base is fiercely protected by the American military, but that didn't stop the Frag Hero team from going there in search of answers (and Pokémon). They didn't find any evidence for the X-Files; instead, they found something stranger—empty gyms! Of course they claimed them. On their journey they cataloged the stops and gyms they found while hunting for Pokémon. They caught a Ponyta outside the base.

Sometimes even the name of a PokéStop is creepy, like the Slide of Never Ending Agony.

Not to be outdone, YouTubers SuperMega checked the base, too, and found "mysterious" server crashes whenever they got near. Is the US government trying to stop people from finding Mew? Only time will tell.

The town near Area 51 is filled with alien-themed PokéStops like Alien Cowboy Mural, UFO Sculpture, and the Extraterrestrial Highway. Just outside the site is a PokéStop humorously titled Alien Research Center. If you go to this conspiracy-rich spot, don't press your luck by breaking the law and illegally entering the base. Claiming you're there on behalf of Professor Willow won't help you get out of trouble.

Alkimos Shipwreck · Perth, Australia

To get to the *Alkimos* Shipwreck PokéStop off the coast of Perth, you will need a boat, and one that is better built than what lies there. What is presently a popular diving location was once a merchant ship that wrecked more than once. In a comedy of errors, this ship crashed and got repaired three times before finally succumbing to Davy Jones' Locker.

What makes this ship so creepy is that sailors who served on the ship reported screams at night and a feeling that they were being watched. On more than one occasion, sailors prematurely evacuated the ship before their service was

Just outside the site is the Alien Research Center PokéStop. If you go to this conspiracy-rich spot, don't press your luck by illegally entering the base.

complete. Other ships claim that they've heard mysterious and threatening broadcasts coming from the *Alkimos*. As a result, the ship has acquired a reputation for being haunted. When you do head out to see it, perhaps the much safer and less haunted S.S. *Ann* will be your boat of choice.

Säter Mental Institution · Säter, Sweden

This is a Snorlax nest! For whatever reason, the city of Säter attracts the sleeping Pokémon. We think it has to do with the abandoned mental institution in the area. Snorlax sleep in inconvenient locations on forest paths, so it might be the remoteness of this area that attracts them.

If you are able to avoid any unwanted Snorlax, then you can explore the abandoned mental institution. The building has the creepy feel to it that only old mental institutions can provide. Being in the middle of Nowhere, Sweden, ups the spooky atmosphere. If the abandoned area seems too creepy, head over to the Mentalvårdsmuseum PokéStop at the Mental Health Museum. Please let us know if you notice a connection between Snorlax and other old mental institutions in your area.

Aradale Mental Hospital · Ararat, Australia

Abandoned after 140 years of use, the sprawling Aradale Mental Hospital feels more like a ghost town than a medical center. Roughly thirteen thousand people died here while the hospital was operating. You'll feel small when walking through the main building's cavernous interior. On the plus side, the big space gives you plenty of opportunities to spot an errant Haunter or Dusknoir.

Pokémon trainers don't need to fear the ghosts in Australia as much as the criminals. In New South Wales (as in other parts of the world), criminals have accosted PoGo players. If you hear a spooky noise, it could be a ghost, or it could be a mugger. Be aware of your surroundings!

THERE ARE POKÉSTOPS IN EVERY CORNER OF GERMANY'S FRANKENSTEIN CASTLE.

Frankenstein Castle · Darmstadt, Germany

Yes, *that* Frankenstein. Inspired by this castle, Mary Shelley wrote *Frankenstein*, and now the frightening structure serves as good hunting grounds for the haunting type. There are PokéStops in nearly every corner of this dank castle, from the living insect wall (Insekten-Wohnwand) in the south to the bizarre, giant ear trumpet on the north grounds (Hörtrichter). One can only imagine what experiments occurred at this place.

Just like a character in Shelley's novel, you can battle a monster here, and that's whichever Pokémon is holding the Burg Frankenstein gym. If that gym is too tough, you can always take on one of the other two gyms on the castle grounds.

ALL THE SITES OF THE JACK THE RIPPER MURDERS HAVE POKÉSTOPS NEAR THEM.

Jack the Ripper Tour · London, England

Jack the Ripper was a serial killer who murdered at least five women in London near the end of the nineteenth century. He's believed to be one of the first recorded serial killers, and hopefully you won't be his ghost's next victim when you go on a Jack the Ripper tour. For an immersive experience, we suggest taking one of the many walking tours offered in the East End.

For a creepy PoGo experience, you can merge the horrors of history with modern gameplay. All the sites of the murders have seemingly innocuous PokéStops near them. Where Mary Ann Nichols was murdered now stands a building and PokéStop known as the Lord Napier, which seems banal despite the location's significance. An odd-looking piece of art, Pink Ear Sculpture, is the closest PokéStop to where Annie Chapman met her demise. A nice statue named *Goodman's Fields Horses* stands beside the site of Elizabeth Stride's murder. Jack the Ripper killed Catherine

Even the art of the Westfjords is spooky

Eddowes near the current PokéStop at Sir John Cass Foundation School. And Mary Jane Kelly's murder site now has a statue with a PokéStop called *Madonna Incoroneta*.

The tour really highlights the disconnect between the suffering of these individuals and the way we now enjoy the same environment. For more cognitive dissonance, when you're done the tour, you can hit up Secret London to find the next Pokémon Go Rave!

Westfjords · Iceland

This inhospitable part of Iceland is unwelcoming, cold, and where criminals were sent for centuries. According to Icelandic

TRACKER TIP
Collect fifty ghost-type Pokémon for the silver Hex Maniac medal.

sagas, the Westfjords is the residence of witches, ghouls, and the like. Despite our warnings, you may find yourself drawn to the Westfjords. One of the most popular attractions there is the Museum of Icelandic Sorcery and Witchcraft, where you can learn about the place's mysterious and frightening history. This is a good entry point to the vast, rocky, and frozen haunted lands.

This tradition of the Westfjords being a destination for the supernatural continues. Throughout the peninsula you can find PokéStops of creepy cravings (Ísafjörður Víking in the Woods) and seemingly endless trails, like Naustahvilt. (If walking it sounds too scary, don't worry: the PokéStop is at the entrance.) Even the art of the Westfjords is spooky—check out the PokéStop Hand Statue in Súðavík, for example. One trainer has seen a Gloom in these parts, so even the Pokémon know what's going on.

ARTISTIC PLACES

Catch some culture and Pokémon at the same time! Public art beautifies our communities and inspires both its inhabitants and visitors. Chancing upon interesting public art can make your day. Art reflects the time and place it was created, so stopping and enjoying the local art can help you better understand the world

DON'T MISS THE POKÉSTOP

AT ELVIS PRESLEY'S

GRACELAND MANSION

around you. When visiting a new city, take a look at the local galleries. The Centre Pompidou in Paris has three PokéStops, while across the English Channel Mr. Mime has apparently been spotted between the Warhols and the Pollocks at the Tate Modern in London. Argyle Fine Art, a gallery in Halifax, Nova Scotia, even hosted an art-themed Pokémon hunt in the city. Check out other popular art galleries and museums around the world for similar programs and stops.

For the musically inclined Pokémon players out there, we recommend visiting one of the festivals described in this chapter. Music fans will also be pleased to hear that Pinsir has been seen in **Strawberry Fields**, the area of New York's Central Park that honors John Lennon. You can wear your blue suede shoes to another PokéStop—**Elvis Presley's mansion, Graceland**—or dress up for a night out with Pokémon at the **Sydney Opera House**.

Bookworms can find Pokémon hiding in many unique literary locations, as well. Check out the **British Library**, which is home to over 150 million documents and who knows how many Pokémon. While in London, muggles and PoGo trainers alike

When visiting a new city, take a look at the local galleries.

can also head to **King's Cross Station** to catch Nidoran, Drowzee, Pidgey, Rattata and the Hogwarts Express at platform 9 and ¾. Go across the pond to get to another one: **Walden Pond**, Massachusetts, inspiration for Henry David Thoreau's *Walden: or, Life in the Woods* and location of at least two PokéStops. Whether your travel budget allows a trip to the PokéStops at Macbeth's **Inverness Castle** or only bus fare to your local library, you're bound to come across some Pokémon on the way. Here are some of the most bizarre artistic Pokémon locations we've found.

Kindlifresser · Bern, Switzerland

Kindlifresser is a fountain featuring a statue perched atop a tall column surrounded by bears. Here you'll find a Poké-Stop, but the fountain has been drawing spectators for years due to its unique nature. You can instantly find out what makes this monument strange by translating the German name: Child Eater. Nobody knows the true story behind the statue, but there is speculation it was built as a warning to the Jewish population or as a monument to Kronos, who ate his god-children in a Greek myth.

Vigeland Park · Oslo, Norway

Norway is home to an entire park dedicated to the work of Gustav Vigeland, a prolific artist who spent his life exploring the human form. His collected works can be found in Vigeland Park, now also a local hot spot for Pokémon catching, according to Norwegian radio station, NRK. Don't be thrown off, though, if the names of the sculptures and Poké-Stops don't always match. One piece is called *Man Attacked by Babies*, while the PokéStop is simply Baby Fighter. It's a strange park and worth checking out for the unique collection of monuments to the human body.

"WITH ALL THE NEGATIVITY IN THE WORLD, I THINK THAT PLAYING POKÉMON GO IS UNIFYING."

Trainer Ash Fedanzo

Cloud Gate, Millennium Park · Chicago, USA

If you're in downtown Chicago, you may come across a giant bean. Neither you nor your Pokémon will be able to eat it, though; it's part of Millennium Park. The art installation, nicknamed the Bean, is a mirrored metal object that looks like an inflated legume ready to pop at any moment! Visitors are able to walk completely around and through an arched section of the sculpture. *Cloud Gate*, which is the bean's actual name, is not only art—it's also a Pokémon gym. The gym saw a lot of battles when roughly five thousand trainers showed up for one of the first PoGo launch parties.

LOOK UP
Treat your eyes and ears to the PokéStop at Sibelius Hall, a beautiful concert venue in Lahti, Finland.

Anish Kapoor, the artist who created *Cloud Gate*, wants his work to spur reflection about the ways we as a culture identify with what's around us. Playing Pokémon Go seems to have a similar effect to the one Kapoor intended for his installation. At the Chicago launch party, Pokémon trainer Ash Fedanzo put it this way in a comment to *Tech Crunch*: "With all the negativity in the world, I think that playing Pokémon Go is unifying." PoGo brings us into a space and makes us see it (and everything and everyone in it) in a new light—just like passing through *Cloud Gate* does.

Callejón de Hamel · Havana, Cuba

Another place where one can pass through the art is farther south in Havana, Cuba. In Havana you can walk along Callejón de Hamel, an entire street dedicated to local art and the celebration of Afro-Cuban culture, where you're even invited into the artists' studios to see them work.

Look for the PokéStop of the same name. This location is also a shrine to Santeria, where rituals are often performed; please be respectful of the people and customs. Nearby, another aptly named PokéStop awaits your spin: the Artist Salvador Gonzales Sculpture, named after the progenitor of the street's art.

For American trainers, getting to Cuba can be a challenge as a result of exclusionary policies put in place by the US during the Cold War. Thankfully, the embargo on Cuba is loosening; hopefully, Americans will soon be able to catch Pokémon as easily on the island nation as they can in another place greatly impacted by the Cold War: Berlin.

Berlin Wall · Germany

The Cold War split the city into East and West Berlin. The public art on both sides of the wall from that era shows a clear difference in cultural styles from one side of the city to the other. The east features more brutalism, while the west displays a plethora of styles from the mid- to late-twentieth century. To see this in person, head to the grouping of PokéStops around the Stasi Museum on the east side and compare the public art around there to the Neue Nationalgalerie in the west.

The remaining sections of the Berlin Wall itself are the best example of the artistic divide. The wall extended around the entirety of West Berlin and became a symbol of repression and exclusion. The west-facing wall was covered in graffiti, while the east-facing wall looked like a blank slate. Today you can walk along the path of the wall, finding PokéStops and gyms like Wallfahrt Rocketman. Artists have reclaimed the wall by covering both sides in art.

THANKS TO THE POPULARITY OF POGO, YOU CAN FIND GREAT WORKS OF POKÉART TO HANG ON YOUR WALLS.

Pikachu Statue · New Orleans, USA

Our favorite small and absurd monument is in New Orleans, where anonymous artists erected a statue of Pikachu shortly after PoGo was released. One local, Jennifer Curry, told the Associated Press, "The kids are fans and I'm just kind of amused at how something so heavy can appear so quickly." In a few weeks the statue disappeared as quickly as it had appeared. The statue was removed because of vandalism and too much wear and tear, the anonymous artists told the *Times Picayune* in an email. Their efforts to "enlist [the Coliseum Square Association's] help to possibly achieve some permanent, positive change for the neighborhood" will pay off in September 2016, when the statue will be auctioned off, with proceeds going towards the improvement of green spaces in the district. For updates on the statue, check out #POKÉMONU-MENT. There aren't many video games

In a few weeks, the statue disappeared as quickly as it had appeared.

that have statues in public spaces, so that's all the more reason to celebrate this one.

Yarn Pokémon · Lewisville, Texas, USA

Keep an eye out for surprising little pieces of art while you're visiting PokéStops, because you never know what you'll find. In Lewisville, Texas, you may discover little crocheted Pokémon made by local artist Nichole Dunigan. The adorable little guys look exactly how you'd think they would—right down to the Tangela. Her work inspired the #CrochetGO Facebook group, and now people all over the world are leaving treats for trainers to find. One artist even filled a Magikarp with actual candy and left it for other trainers! For tips on how to make what are perhaps the cutest Pokémon ever, join the group.

Graffiti Alley, Your Town

If it's too hard for you to travel to these faraway places, you can always find art in your town. Graffiti alleys exist all over the world and it's likely you'll be able to find PokéStops in them. Bright and cheerful, not dark and scary, these alleys just happen to be places where local graffiti artists can throw up their art.

Try your hand at creating street art by drawing your favorite Pokémon in sidewalk chalk.

Graffiti researcher (yes, that's his job!) Lachlan MacDowall in **Melbourne, Australia**, was impressed by how PoGo makes use of street and public art. "In my brief test run in Fitzroy, about half of the Pokéstops were spray-painted examples of street art or graffiti. Others were public artworks that I rarely notice, such as Giuseppe Raneri's *Sun* sculpture on Brunswick Street." PoGo doesn't just get players to take a closer look at the art world around them; it gets artists to do so, as well! MacDowall encourages us to think about both

TRACKER TIP
For a punny time, unlock the Fairy Tale Girl medal at a literary location!

Pokémon Go and graffiti in new ways: "The Pokémon craze shows us how graffiti and street art are already forms of social media, their own kind of massive, multiplayer game, with their own sites and rewards hidden across the city."

If you are exploring your own neighborhood in search of Pokémon, you should stop every now and then to enjoy the art that is around you. You might learn something new about your own community.

Music Festivals

Australia is home to **Splendour in the Grass,** which hosted the first ever Pokémon hunt during a music festival. The organizers made this announcement: "Meet at the Amphitheatre stage at 3:15 p.m. on the Friday, watch DMA's, and then let's go catch those little f***ers." Their enthusiasm was palpable.

In the middle of a lake in Hungary you can feel the beat drop at the annual **Balaton Sound festival.** The event features two thousand square meters (half a mile) of venue space right on the lake—a primo way to listen to your electronic dance music and catch water Pokémon. On the shore of Lake Balaton, you can find a PokéStop with a picture of musical sheets called "Hangjegy," which translates simply as "note."

Vice columnist Kyle Kramer wrote that, when attending music festivals, connectivity is an issue: "It turns out that all the usual phone service troubles that plague music festivals or any other gathering of twenty thousand people in the same two-block radius are as much a roadblock for augmented reality gaming as they are with getting off fire tweets." So perhaps sticking with smaller events is a safer bet.

LOOK UP
Keep an eye out for art festivals like the Prague Quadrennial and Art Basel.

There are probably small events happening around where you live *right now.* Embrace the spirit of PoGo and get out there and explore festivals near you. When you do find them, please share with your local PoGo players. PoGo is a game that gets people out and exploring. The next logical step is to engage those spaces in new ways. Who knows, maybe you'll get inspired to start an event based off of some cool PokéStop you find!

The Balaton Sound festival

is a primo way to listen to

electronic dance music and

catch water Pokémon

FAMOUS PLACES

Every trainer has a must-do list of gyms, whether it includes Viridian City or another exciting place. There's likely to be at least one famous location on your way, so take the time on your journey to enjoy these wonders. You can explore the ancient history in

Egypt or go more modern and reach for the stars at NASA. Famous spots span the globe, and so do those gyms!

Pyramids · Giza, Egypt

One of the most famous ancient wonders of the world is the pyramid complex at Giza. It contains some great Pokéstops and gyms, like the Sphinx, Kephren's Pyramid, Mykerinos Pyramid, and even the Top of Cheops Pyramid, which is probably the hardest to get to. The gyms are fought over by tourists and locals alike, despite the fact the game has not yet been released in Egypt.

According to *CairoScene*, PokéMaster Skot Thayer and his team set off to "loot Egypt's historical landmarks of their (digital) valuables just like pasty European colonialists would" and discovered eight Pokémon in their visits to the pyramids, the Egyptian Museum, and the Citadel of Saladin. Referencing a photo of an Onix next to a statue, they write, "Nobody knows exactly how the pharaohs built their amazing monuments... [but] I'd have to say rock-type Pokémon had something to do with it."

Even when visiting the safer tourist attractions like the pyramids, be conscious of where you're pointing your camera in the security-conscious state. *Al Arabiya* reported that, during a press conference, a former National Research Center official warned players that PoGo "tracks his way of living... where he lives, the style of his house and the number of residents without the need to send spies."

TRACKER TIP
Location matters! Some Pokémon can only be caught in certain regions.
• **Mr. Mime: Europe**
• **Tauros: North America**
• **Kangaskhan: Australia**
• **Farfetch'd: Asia**

Where ancient Greeks debated politics, you can battle Pokémon at the Doric Stoa gym.

The Acropolis of Athens · Greece

The Acropolis captures the best qualities of ancient Greek culture, for it's a symbol of democracy, philosophy, and the pursuit of the arts. Where ancient Greeks debated politics, you can battle Pokémon at the Doric Stoa gym. In the Acropolis you'll find shrines to Poseidon and Zeus, which makes it a great spot to catch water- and fighting-type Pokémon.

Touring this UNESCO site, you will find buildings that sound like they are Pokémon themselves. There's the Propylaea (the entrance), Arrephorion (lodgings), and the Erechtheum (shrine to Athena and Poseidon)—all of which have PokéStops! After you enjoy the history of the Acropolis, you can take a twenty-minute walk to meet other players of PoGo at Syntagma Square.

LOOK UP
You can see intricate marble carvings from the Parthenon in the British Museum in London.

Taj Mahal · Agra, India

The Taj Mahal is a monument to love that attracts people the world over. In the city of Agra, this stunning complex continues to awe visitors hundreds of years after its construction in 1653. The complex was commissioned by Mughal emperor Shah Jahan in the memory of his favorite wife, who died giving birth.

On a popular Indian tech website, Digit, Robert Sovereign-Smith wrote a column titled "Pokémon No"; he's obviously not a fan. "I can just imagine people running up and down the gardens of the Taj Mahal flinging virtual balls at cartoons, just ruining the experience for everyone else," he wrote. The complex includes many sacred buildings, including a mosque as the centerpiece, so remember to respect the grounds when you are there.

BATTLE AT THE TAJ MAHAL'S TWO GYMS, OR VISIT NUMEROUS POKÉSTOPS IN THE GARDENS.

There are two gyms on the grounds that claim to represent the Taj Mahal. The immaculate Taj Mahal, Agra, is one; the other is Taj Mahal Shining in Evening Sun. You can battle at either one, or visit numerous PokéStops in the gardens.

Machu Picchu · Cuzco Region, Peru

For an ancient site, Machu Picchu has an amazing number of PokéStops. You can spin the Sun Gate, tap the Temple of the Condor, and of course, hit up the eponymous Machu Picchu PokéStop. It's as if the Incan builders were waiting for PoGo. At the entrance you can battle at the gym. You can catch a lot of Pokémon at the Incan wonder. One reporter for Peru.com found that not only can Pikachu appear on the Intihuatana, but also his friends Nidoran, Zubat, and Pidgey, among others. The confluence of so many PokéStops, spawning Pokémon, the gym, and the gorgeous scenery, accompanied by the history of the site, make Machu Picchu a must for any global trainer.

FOR AN

ANCIENT SITE,

MACHU PICCHU

HAS AN AMAZING

NUMBER OF

POKÉSTOPS.

Panama Canal · Panama

If you are curious about seeing industrial transportation and catching Pokémon at the same time, then head to the Panama Canal. Making this seventy-seven-kilometer (forty-eight-mile) canal through the heart of Panama was one of the most difficult engineering challenges ever undertaken. Thanks to the canal, ships have a shortcut around the southern tip of Chile. Visitors to the canal will want to head to the touristy PokéStops like the Miraflores Lock Mural, Anclas De Ciudad Del Saber, or the Pedro Miguel Locks Plaque.

The expansion of the Panama Locks and the presence of mobile games like Pokémon Go have led the owners of the canal to contemplate banning cell access. Just like you shouldn't play and drive, navigators shouldn't ship and play. When asked why they are considering this policy, an official said he's unaware "if any Canal employee was playing Pokémon Go on his or her mobile device," but he added that "we cannot give ourselves the luxury of having a distraction."

Shangri-La, Yunnan, China

First mentioned in the 1933 book *Lost Horizon* by James Hilton, this mythical city is said to be found somewhere in the Himalayas. Shangri-La is like the Towers of Ecruteak (in northern Johto) at their prime and is claimed to be a city of peace and knowledge, providing immortality for its inhabitants. So many movies, books, and video games have referenced the utopian city that, in 1995, a Chinese city in Yunnan province changed its name to Shangri-La to attract tourists. There you can enjoy a PokéStop at the beautiful lookout over Tiger Leaping Gorge. Both the gorge and Pudacuo National Park are said to have inspired the book. Finding the mythical city, however, remains a challenge, just like figuring out how to play the game behind the great firewall of China.

Get the Battle Girl medal by winning gym battles at famous locations.

BATTLE OTHER TRAINERS FOR CONTROL OF THE WHITE HOUSE AT THE NORTH FOUNTAIN GYM.

White House · Washington, DC, USA

Every four years, a battle occurs for who gets to reside in the White House. The odds of being part of that presidential bout are slim; luckily, there's a gym there. You can battle for control with other trainers at the White House North Fountain. Of course, because it's where the president lives, the gym has been used for political messages. One of the first owners of the gym used a Pidgeot named MERICA, later renamed THANKS OBAMA. Not to be outdone, Joshua Shull then placed a Magikarp named THE DONALD. Shull told *Kotaku* his reasons: "I wanted to do something unique, something memorable, something that would maybe both communicate something valuable while being humorous. Thus, The Donald." He went on to say, "There's always a huge crowd of tourists in front of the place normally; now just half of them are fighting for the gym." So get there early! Then, after battling, enjoy the plethora of PokéStops and a nice walk along the Washington Mall.

Kennedy Space Center · Cape Canaveral, Florida, USA

Can astronauts capture Pokémon while in space? Shortly after the game was released, curious trainers took to Twitter to find out. One of them was Meg (@apostitute), who asked NASA, "Is there a #PokemonGo gym on the moon and if so, can you confirm for me what team has claimed it? Please and thanks." When the *Verge* reached out to NASA to solve this mystery once and for all, they received the following response: "Unfortunately, it is not possible for the astronauts to play. While there is a small number of smartphones available on the space station, the crew uses them for science activities but not for personal use. The smartphones and other mobile devices on station (tablets) also do not have Internet connectivity."

Despite this disappointing news, back on Earth, the Kennedy Space Center Visitor Complex in Cape Canaveral, Florida, does have three gyms and a lot of PokéStops. Obviously we need to keep an eye out for the tricky Team Rocket, but there is a friendly Team Rocket at NASA that is constantly contributing to science. Check out the Star Seekers Mural and the Space Station Mural PokéStops. To find a gym, head over to the Space Shuttle Atlantis or the Visitor Center. Apparently, some visitors at this busy tourist attraction have spotted Krabby and Rattata.

At NASA, check out the the Star Seekers Mural and the Space Station Mural PokéStops.

We hope that the NASA team changes their policy before the astronauts blast off again to Mars. Then they can start placing some interplanetary PokéStops and gyms along the way! Presently, playing on Mars would be challenging.

If your phone's reception is as bad on Earth as it is on Mars, preload PokéStops before you get to them. Just tap your phone before it's in range.

Nintendo Headquarters · Kyoto, Japan

Why not make a pilgrimage to the place where it all started? The original Pokémon game was created by Nintendo and two other companies. Players of Red and Blue probably remember playing on an original GameBoy. Today players can go to Nintendo's headquarters in Kyoto, Japan, and catch Pokémon in real life, thanks to Niantic and Nintendo's teamwork on PoGo. There's no museum—or anything, really—for tourists at Nintendo's offices, but not far away from the Nintendo headquarters is a gym, and there's a small park nearby with two PokéStops. What better place than here to catch a Pikachu?

World's Fair Sites

The concept of a World's Fair started in the industrial age and continues today. Although they are now known as Expos, they still are collections of the best technology of the era. Since the beginning, they have left a trail of impressive buildings the world over. Unbeknownst to the original planners of the Expos, they also left a trail of magnificent PokéStops for us modern-day travelers.

The famous **Crystal Palace** in London from the 1851 World's Fair now has a collection of PokéStops on its grounds, most using a variation of its name. In New York, there are a few PokéStops located around the fairgrounds of the 1939 World's Fair in **Flushing Meadows–Corona Park**. At the site of the 1967 World's Fair in **Montreal**, today there is a race course, an island, and a geodesic dome, where trainers can battle and catch Pokémon.

The grounds are peppered with PokéStops and gyms where international pavilions once stood.

The 1988 Expo in Brisbane left a mark on the city in the form of an 88-meter- (289-foot-) tall spire—the **Skyneedle**. Trainers in Brisbane meet on the former Expo grounds to start their monthly walks. Posting in the Brisbane PoGo group, Mykal

Hinton writes: "Start at southbank. Everyone parks and meets up at the pub. Have some jugs, then we start."

In 2010, **Shanghai** hosted the largest World's Fair with a land area of 5.28 square kilometers (2.02 square miles) dedicated to the event. Just walking the site will help you hatch eggs! The grounds are peppered with PokéStops and gyms where international pavilions once stood.

Olympic Sites

Every two years, athletes gather to compete with one another by performing feats of strength and agility at the Olympics. The modern Olympics (1896–present) have left a trail of landmarks for us to explore, as each host city has invested billions in new facilities. Indeed, every city that hosted the Olympics has PokéStops named after some of the locations. You can find these sites all over the globe, from Dynamo Stadium in Moscow (1980 Olympics) to Olympic Park in Seoul (1988 Olympics) and even as far back as the Wooneenheid Zaanstraat in Antwerp (1920 Olympics).

Some Olympic sites have been left abandoned, like those in Athens and Sarajevo. In Beijing and Atlanta, the baseball stadiums were demolished after the games. Interestingly, some PokéStops are named after their former use, like Olympic Rings Pavilion in **Beijing**.

In the first summer of PoGo, the game caught on during the Rio Olympics. When Canadian gold medalist Penny Oleksiak was asked what she aspired to do next, she said, "I want to catch them all." She added, "Well, I just crossed off the gold medal at the Olympics... I have to do the Pokémon one now."

Some Olympic sites have been left abandoned, like those in Athens and Sarajevo.

URBAN PLACES

T he United Nations has reported that over half of humankind lives in urban areas for the first time in recorded history. Anybody who has tried catching Pokémon in rural areas knows all too well that cities are where most of the Pokémon are, too. Because the game uses sponsored locations and user-generated content to create destinations, the density of the PokéStops and gyms reflects the actual population. Rural players, now's your chance to start a new life in a new city; the game does encourage exploration of physical space, after all. From bustling transportation hubs to sprawling university campuses and urban parks, this chapter highlights some of the hot spots for Pokémon in cities all over the world.

New York City Subway · USA

Transit systems are essential for quickly getting around a major city, and busy stations are great places to find electric Pokémon. Stations that are also landmarks are even better, because they draw out dragon Pokémon, too. One of the most well-known transportation systems is in New York City, which appropriately has a gym at **Grand Central Terminal** and PokéStops at all major stations. Weary commuters and curious tourists alike find Grand Central's main concourse remarkable, so pause during your search to look at its iconic four-faced brass clock and elaborate astronomical ceiling. For a few weeks in 1957, the main concourse also hosted a nine-meter- (sixty-three-foot-) tall Redstone

Nearly two million passengers travel daily through Tokyo's Shibuya Station, which contains or is close to at least two gyms and a dozen PokéStops. One stop away sits Harajuku Station, which is more about the stylish youth that hang out around than its three PokéStops. This station could be called the most fashionable stop in the world!

missile, which was displayed to cheer Americans up after the Soviets launched Sputnik. The rocket is gone now, but the crowds remain—watch that they don't run you over as you hunt for Pokémon.

Paris Métro · France
If you're walking the streets of Paris you will inevitably see one of the iconic Métro entrances, and odds are that it contains a PokéStop. At the PokéStop Métro Louvre–Rivoli, you can see one of the famous entrances designed by Hector Guimard. Inside, you can marvel at the unique decor of one of Paris Métro's thirty themed stations. This one features replicas of Louvre masterpieces. Other favorites include:

- Bastille station's scenes from the French Revolution and artifacts from the former prison

- Assemblée Nationale station's murals of deputies in silhouette

- Arts et Métiers station's copper interior, designed to look like the inside of a submarine

- Parmentier station's potato exhibits, tractor seats, and green trellises, all celebrating the work of a French scientist who promoted this humble food source

After touring these stations, check out the glass beaded arches at the **Métro Palais Royal** entrance, where you will also find a gym of the same name.

Is there an abandoned submarine in your neighborhood? Two Dutch trainers discovered one and a Nidoran hiding inside!

London Underground · England

London is home to the oldest underground railway (1863), known locally as the Tube. Surprisingly, the busiest station, Waterloo, has no gyms! There are eight PokéStops, though, including the Waterloo Station Clock and an artistic PokéStop beneath the tracks on Leake Street: Banksy graffiti. If you want to see a beautiful Art

So far, cruise ships haven't been good hunting grounds for Pokémon, but the ports are another story. Check out Bayfront Park, near the Port of Miami, for Tentacool, Doduo, Dodrio, Staryu, and others. Try Baltimore Inner Harbor for Magikarp, Gyarados, and Poliwhirl.

Deco station, head to the Charles Holden–designed Southgate station. While enjoying the architecture, you can spin the PokéStop at the entrance. You know the Pokémon Go craze has caught on when the London Underground staff uses it to explain earlier transit delays. "We apologize for yesterday's power failure," they wrote on a sign. "This was due to someone capturing the station Pikachu." A drawing of the popular Pokémon accompanied the message that had many commuters smiling and tweeting.

San Francisco Ferry Building and Cable Cars · USA

Above ground and on the West Coast of the United States, San Francisco, California, has the iconic Ferry Building on the Embarcadero, which has busy docks with commuters and tourists alike using the facility. Completed in 1898, the Beaux Arts–style building has a gym named after its famous, 75-meter- (245-foot-) tall clock tower and multiple PokéStops, like the Gandhi Monument. After visiting the Ferry Building, ride San Francisco's most

"We apologize for yesterday's power failure. This was due to someone capturing the station Pikachu."

famous form of transportation: the cable car. Hop on a Powell/Hyde cable car near Ghirardelli Square and, as it reaches the top of the hill, enjoy the view of Lombard Street, "the world's crookedest street" and Alcatraz Island. At the Powell Street Station terminus, hit the gym named Cable Car Turnaround and the nearby PokéStops.

University of British Columbia (UBC) · Vancouver, Canada

Normal Pokémon show up at university and college campuses around the world. Lucky students can study Pokémon under Professor Elm, and the rest of us can try to catch the Pokémon in the wild. Thankfully, places of higher learning are rife with all sorts of Pokémon. Compared to surrounding areas, these institutions have a higher concentration of gyms and PokéStops.

The UBC campus has more PokéStops than the nearby Vancouver community of Kitsilano. According to "The Complete UBC Guide to Pokémon GO," some students have even

For a longer ferry journey you can head to Dubrovnik, Croatia. The city is seeing an influx of tourists thanks to *Game of Thrones* (the scenes in King's Landing are filmed here), so you may want to take the boat for a less crowded experience. There is one gym and three PokéStops at the port, including the aptly named Luka Dubrovnik PokéStop.

STAY IN SCHOOL: UNIVERSITIES HAVE A HIGHER CONCENTRATION OF GYMS AND POKÉSTOPS.

planted lures near classrooms so that, when they're stuck inside during long classes, "everyone in a lecture can reap the rewards." "Just be sure to at least *try* and pay attention in class, though," the guide adds. Koerner's Pub on campus is also celebrating the game by giving out Instinct, Mystic, and Valor team-themed shots if you take a screenshot of yourself capturing Pokémon in the pub. Two interesting Pokémon gyms on campus can be found at the World War II searchlight tower on Vancouver's famous, clothing-optional Wreck Beach and at the huge *Asiatic Head* sculpture between UBC's Music Building and Frederic Lasserre Building.

University of Cambridge · England

Universities across the ocean exhibit the same pattern of high concentrations of gyms and PokéStops that we see in North American universities and colleges. "Cambridge. Steeped in history and now peppered with Pokémon," the university's account tweeted in mid-July. For the *Tab*,

Randeep Nag writes, "In a post-Brexit 2016 and as a Cambridge student, this game and its lovable little critters are the last remnants of my childhood and provide solace from the grim reality of the world around us and the reading list that I'm supposed to be plowing through." Although Randeep recommends several places on campus where trainers may find success, he also speculates about the game "encouraging people to visit other colleges to see what creatures lurk there," resulting in both "intercollege rivalry" and limitless "procrastination possibilities." During a study break, check out the PokéStop at the River Cam.

"This game and its lovable little critters are the last remnants of my childhood."

University of Idaho · Moscow, Idaho, USA

For a truly in-depth Pokémon learning experience, you should head to the land of potatoes. The University of Idaho has a course in which you actually have to play PoGo to pass! The course, called Pop Culture Games, focuses on ways that games are changing culture. "This app does more than let you shoot a Poké Ball," instructor Steven Bird told the *University of Idaho News*. "You get to adventure around, seeing different things, being active, seeing the sun. It allows you to move in large groups and a team. You get not only physical activity, but you also get team building and leadership."

Central Park · New York City, USA

Urban parks are great places to look for Pokémon. Only five days after the game's release, the popular New York website Gothamist ran an article titled "The NYC Pokémon Go Zombie Apocalypse Is upon Us." You might laugh at that headline now, and it is hyperbolic, but that first weekend hordes of people playing PoGo descended upon Central Park, running around trying to get to the good

lures and the rare spawns, and generally just having a good time. To an outside observer, it looked like chaos. You may have seen the infamous Vaporeon stampede video that was making the rounds online. One PoGo trainer wrote, "Sometimes there were more Pokémon players than non-Pokémon players in areas of the park."

Located in the middle of Manhattan, Central Park is no stranger to new trends. At the turn of the last century, it wasn't augmented reality that was causing such a commotion; instead, it was something that is now a familiar sight in any city: bicycles. Back in the day, park officials reacted to the trend by restricting cyclists so as to "avoid all possible opposition from

Are your feet sore from all that walking? Pedicabs are a popular choice for Pokémon trainers in Central Park!

NEW YORK'S

CENTRAL PARK

CONTAINS OVER

HALF THE

POKÉMON IN

THE GAME.

IN HYDE PARK, LOOK FOR POKÉMON BY THE DIANA, PRINCESS OF WALES MEMORIAL FOUNTAIN.

the public," according to NYC Parks history. The "wheel-men," as they were called, had to register with the Parks Department and wear a badge with a license number on their chest, and they were not allowed to blow whistles or bugles while riding. Today, the city embraces the arrival of PoGo players to the park. The NYPD wishes players luck on their adventures: "Have fun AND stay safe. Good luck in your quest, and happy hatching, trapping, and training at the Pokémon gym!" Adam Wennick has started leading free safaris through Central Park. (He kindly asks for a donation to the Alzheimer's Foundation.) "At last count," he writes, "Central Park contains over half the Pokémon in the game. With lakes, fields, woods, and more, Central Park is the perfect home for all variations. It's time to come catch yours!" The safaris have gotten so popular that Adam enlisted other PoGo trainers to also give tours. Going on this safari is a great way to meet new trainers, explore Central Park, and even learn a little about its famous history.

Hyde Park · London, England

In London, England, there are similar organized safaris happening. Not far from Buckingham Palace is Hyde Park, which has been overrun by PoGo players. The British Tourist Authority even suggests on their website going to the park to catch Pokémon: "Stretching north from Hyde Park Corner to Marble Arch, Hyde Park is a huge island of green among London's busiest shopping streets. It makes a great spot for a picnic, cycle, or Pokémon hunt.

You can often find them hanging about by the Diana, Princess of Wales Memorial Fountain."

Turia Gardens · Valencia, Spain

Another park that's seeing an influx of people is Turia Gardens in Valencia, which is one of the largest urban parks in Spain. The park stretches around the city center from a hub of museums on one end to a zoo on the other. The City of Arts and Sciences museum spawns a Snorlax daily, according to one source using the odd name of Que Pasa Si. Even the Spanish newspaper *El Mundo* lists the museum as one of the best spawning spots in the country. That one site in the park has over six PokéStops itself, with even more that are less than a five-minute walk away. One Valencian blogger walked the entire park and found more Pokémon than he knew what to do with. He wrote that he found Magmar, Goldeen, Omanyte, Vulpix, Oddish, Poliwag, Sandslash, and "*mucho bicho*" (many bugs), as well as other Pokémon.

Parks are great places to get the Gardener, Bird Keeper, and Hiker medals.

Your Local Park

No matter where you are, there is probably a local park to explore. After a lure was placed on a PokéStop in his neighborhood park, one player posted about his positive

Dogs are probably benefiting the most from Pokémon Go, a good excuse for owners to take them on walks. Animal shelters have caught on and are using PoGo to attract more volunteers. Thanks to their Pokémon Go publicity campaign, one shelter in Muncie, Indiana, went from one or two dog walkers a day to 250 in less than a week.

There's a PokéStop called Young Human Entertainment with a picture of generic playground equipment. You might be able to find similar PokéStops in your local park.

experience on a GameFAQs board: "Around twenty people of all ages, genders, and ethnicities [were] talking, joking, and comparing [catches] by the time it was over." PoGo is bringing people into parks who might otherwise not enter the space and enjoy it. There is a PokéStop called Young Human Entertainment with a picture of generic playground equipment. This PokéStop was totally not made by a robot. You might be able to find similar PokéStops in your local park. It's worth checking it out.

Some city parks are swamped with players. If you drive to these parks, be careful about where you leave your car! In **Ottawa, Canada**, $12,000 worth of parking tickets were handed out at a PoGo event. "There were vehicles everywhere," Scott Campbell, program manager for Ottawa's bylaw enforcement unit, told CTV Ottawa. "On the lawns, on the grass, and even [at] the entrances."

If you're heading to popular parks, please be conscious of other people who are also enjoying the space.

If you are heading to popular parks, please be conscious of other people who are also enjoying the space.

In **Sydney, Australia**, there was a problem in Peg Paterson Park with too many trainers not respecting the community, leading to some locals literally water bombing players. On the Sydney PoGo Facebook page, Adam Shalala posted, "The backlash has started. Three hundred of us in Rhodes got water bombed by some resident in the apartments." Not too long after that posting, Niantic removed the PokéStops from Peg Paterson Park, at the community's request.

Location, Location: Tracker Tips

- Would you rather travel by air or by sea? **Capture a Nidoran while in a hot air balloon**, like one trainer did.

- Maybe you could take a rickshaw instead? One company in **Raleigh, North Carolina**, invites you to "incubate and hatch your Pokémon eggs faster" while riding one of their on-demand rickshaws.

- A Pokémon Go vintage scooter tour in **Athens, Greece**, allows you to see the landmarks of this historic city while catching 'em all.

- In **Berlin, Germany**, the newest and biggest train station, Berlin Hauptbahnhof, has no less than three gyms and four PokéStops. *Die Welt* reports that they found a Mr. Mime in the station!

- The Bund area of **Shanghai**'s intense transit system has more stops than most towns do.

- In **Monaco**, you can take an electric boat, the Bateau Bus, across one of the many bays. At one terminus you'll find a statue of Ulysses with a gym.

NATURAL PLACES

A love of nature is at the foundation of the entire Pokémon series. Indeed, the creator of Pokémon, Satoshi Tajiri, told *Time* magazine that his memories of catching bugs during his childhood in rural Japan are what inspired him to make Pokémon in the first place.

With PoGo, the connection to nature is even more visceral; now you can go and catch things in the wild, too!

PoGo has encouraged people to explore the world around them. We love getting some fresh air, so we often head out into natural spaces looking for grass- and ground-type Pokémon.

This chapter takes you from the fiery depths of volcanoes, over roaring waterfalls and white-water rapids, across the vast plains of the prairies, and up steep mountains to summits in the clouds. When out enjoying nature, remember the rule that the most experienced campers live by: take only pictures (and Pokémon) and leave only footprints (but not too many).

Popocatépetl Volcano · Mexico

Fire types spawn around volcanoes, which draws trainers to these explosive mountains. Volcanoes are fascinating geological forms and make for a great hike—at least if it's safe to do so. Fire types do spawn elsewhere, but it's quite the claim to say you caught a Moltres on a volcano!

There is a Magmar nest near an easily accessible volcano in Mexico: Popocatépetl. Its close proximity to Mexico City makes Popocatépetl easy to get to but also particularly dangerous, because if it erupts, it will likely kill millions of people. The active volcano released an ash plume three kilometres (two miles) high in 2016, which sounds scary enough. In the first month of PoGo being released, the volcano has already spewed rocks at players in the nearby city of Puebla. This didn't

Hawaii is also a prime location for catching fire-type Pokémon. Trek to Coconut Island, Hawaii Volcanoes National Park, and Rainbow Falls just to play!

Pokémon fire types spawn around volcanoes, which draws trainers to these explosive mountains.

IF YOU AREN'T USED TO

BEING NEAR A FIERY,

EXPLODING CAULDRON,

POKÉMON HUNTING

NEAR A VOLCANO CAN

BE STRESSFUL.

surprise residents, since the volcano has been active for decades. If you aren't used to being near a fiery, exploding cauldron, then this will be a stressful visit. The city has some downtown gyms with excellent views of Popocatépetl, including a great spot at the ecological park, where trainers regularly gather. Diario Judio wrote, "Magmar makes the rounds every time we see a fumarole of Popo. People in the state of Puebla who approach the volcano could surely capture them."

Masaya Volcano · Nicaragua

Volcanoes are not just hot spots for fire-type Pokémon, as poison types can spawn there, too. In Nicaragua, the Masaya Volcano looks very inviting. Enjoy a nice walk around it, but if the birds aren't there, you should run. Just before an eruption all the birds living around the volcano fly off to the local

town where their arrival warns locals of impending doom. The birds evacuate because they can smell the poison and toxic gases Masaya releases. It happens frequently enough that it's common for the site to be closed down. If you have to make a choice between getting that Weezing or running, we advise running.

Blue Lagoon and Myvatn Nature Baths · Iceland

Going near a volcano is usually enough to catch fire-type Pokémon, and if you find a hot spring nearby, you can likely get some water types, too. For a hot springs and volcano combination, we suggest heading to the land of ice and fire: Iceland. The Blue Lagoon and the Myvatn Nature Baths are hot springs warmed by lava flows beneath the surface. Fans of the show *Game of Thrones* will recognize the Myvatn area as the land north of the wall. Conveniently, you can take one tour focusing on the show, and you can take another one hunting Pokémon! The tour starts in Reykjavik. Remember, playing with fire can blast you off like Team Rocket.

Niagara Falls · Ontario, Canada

Water can appear calm, complete with Magikarp splashing around, but beneath the surface a ferocious Gyarados could be waiting for lunch. It is at once both lovely and capable of destruction. If you head to Niagara Falls, you will be able to see one of the largest and most beautiful waterfalls in the world. Swimming around this area is very dangerous, as the current will take you over the falls. If you survive that, then your next stop is a whirlpool. Whatever you do, don't fall in!

Keep natural areas looking beautiful. Bring an extra bag and collect litter— make the world a little better while playing PoGo.

Another danger in this area is the tacky tourist area on Clifton Hill, where local businesses have caught on that they can use lures to attract customers. The chamber of commerce may see this as a good thing, telling the *St. Catharines Standard* that it's a "pull strategy that gives opportunity to engage new consumers in a different and unique way." But we say save yourself some cash and don't spend time in the city itself. Enjoy the view of the falls, make some good catches, and then get out.

We have found that water-type Pokémon really like the area upstream from the falls and that downstream you will find an odd assortment of Pokémon spawning. A Hitmonchan has been seen on the American side of the falls, and near the hydro power plant on the Canadian side you can find electric Pokémon.

White-Water Rafting in the Poconos · Pennsylvania, USA

There are multiple white-water rafting trips for you to try out, whether you're in America or Australia or Austria! As long as you are able to get reception for your smartphone, you should be able to catch some water Pokémon. In the

Biologists are encouraging trackers to use #PokeBlitz in an effort to identify real-life species that are caught on the app's camera. If you identify a new species, you might get the chance to name it after a Pokémon character. Like the new species of bee discovered this year, called the stem-nesting Charizard.

Poconos, there's a company called Whitewater Challengers that offers rafting and mountain-biking trips that include
Pokémon-hunting advice and stops. Their on-site gym is
clearly a source of contention. On their website, they write
that "right now the PokeGym is under control of a White-
water Challengers' river guide; however, our kitchen staff
is looking to take back control soon." They also report that
trainers have caught Pokémon only at the start and the end
of their rafting route—but maybe you can
change that! Our advice is to wear a life **Collect medals for**
jacket, and at the very least, get some water **catching specific**
protection for your phone. **types of Pokémon,**
like Swimmer for
water types.

Kayaking in Oriental Bay · Wellington, New Zealand

Trainers Lizzy Eden and Kelsey Thomson were out looking for Pokémon and found an unclaimed gym in the middle of Oriental Bay. Eden told the media, "We tried to get close on land, but the game wasn't having a bar of it, so we devised a plan to get a kayak," and so they did. The duo hadn't kayaked since they were kids, but they successfully went out and claimed the gym for Team Mystic. Others saw them kayaking and surmised what was going on; @mrgreatnews tweeted, "Two people, in a kayak. Staring at their phones. #PokemonGO is getting serious."

Mount Everest · Nepal

There are ranges of mountains all over the world that have taken millions of years to form and provide good Pokémon catching grounds. Any good trainer knows about Mt. Moon and how only that mountain can provide the needed Dome and Helix fossils. Older trainers might remember that the place to catch wild Clefairy is in Mt. Moon.

FREE WI-FI ON MT. FUJI MEANS YOU CAN CATCH POKÉMON ALL THE WAY TO THE TOP.

The equivalent of Mt. Moon is Everest. This popular mountain has seen over 270 recorded deaths, making climbing it a very dangerous quest. If PoGo has increased your activity from sedentary to moderate, then you should probably work out a little more before attempting the climb. It's too early to know if there is a PokéStop at the top of the mountain, but we have seen rumors online that there is one. There are also rumors that Articuno spawns there. Nobody has gone to take a look yet. What we do know is that you will want to bring along some fire Pokémon for warmth, at the very least.

Ben Nevis · Scotland

A much smaller mountain in Scotland, Ben Nevis, is an easier climb. Many trainers have made the ascent; one climber (who wants to remain anonymous) claims that she spotted the legendary Zapdos but was unable to capture it. At the summit, Ben Nevis has a gym and a PokéStop , which makes us hopeful that Everest will have the same.

Mount Fuji · Japan

The hiking trails to the top of Mount Fuji are lined with station markers, and some of those markers are PokéStops. Free Wi-Fi was installed on the mountain in 2016, meaning that you can catch Pokémon all the way without worrying about losing your connection. The hardest part of this climb will probably be keeping your phone charged. One hiker, Paul from PokéJungle.net, got to the top and made a horrifying discovery: "I quickly dropped a lure to maximize my chances of finding anything I could. Suddenly, disaster

struck: my battery, which had just been at 69 percent, sank all the way to 1 percent." His sister had an extra battery pack and saved the day.

Fargo, Minnesota, USA

The view from Mt. Moon provides brave climbers with a great vista. For those of us who cannot make the ascent, we can head to more accessible areas known as the prairies. The North American prairies are famous for their flat land and wide-open skies. The area is the bread basket of Canada and the United States. It's also a good place to catch Pokémon while seeing an amazing view. Throughout the prairies, players are getting outside and looking far and wide for Pokémon.

Check out the small town of Gimli, outside of Winnipeg, Canada, suggests Reddit user DiamondKoolaid. Look for a spot near the Viking statue with four overlapping stops.

One trainer reports that nearly all of Fargo's painted bison statues are PokéStops. Kali Bauer tweeted that the Microsoft campus in Fargo is filled with trainers battling as "the gym is literally right in the middle of campus #productivity."

The 2016 Minnesota State Fair fully embraced PoGo and drew trainers to the fair by releasing a special map. The PokéMap shows the fairgrounds, plus it highlights Poké-Stops, gyms, and even charging stations.

Saskatoon, Saskatchewan, Canada

The "Paris of the prairies" is very welcoming to PoGo trainers. The city has been rolling out free public Wi-Fi that trainers can use at the popular Civic Square PokéStop. "We are sitting outside of City Hall in the dark in the evening with a

North America's wide-open prairies are a good place to catch Pokémon while seeing an amazing view.

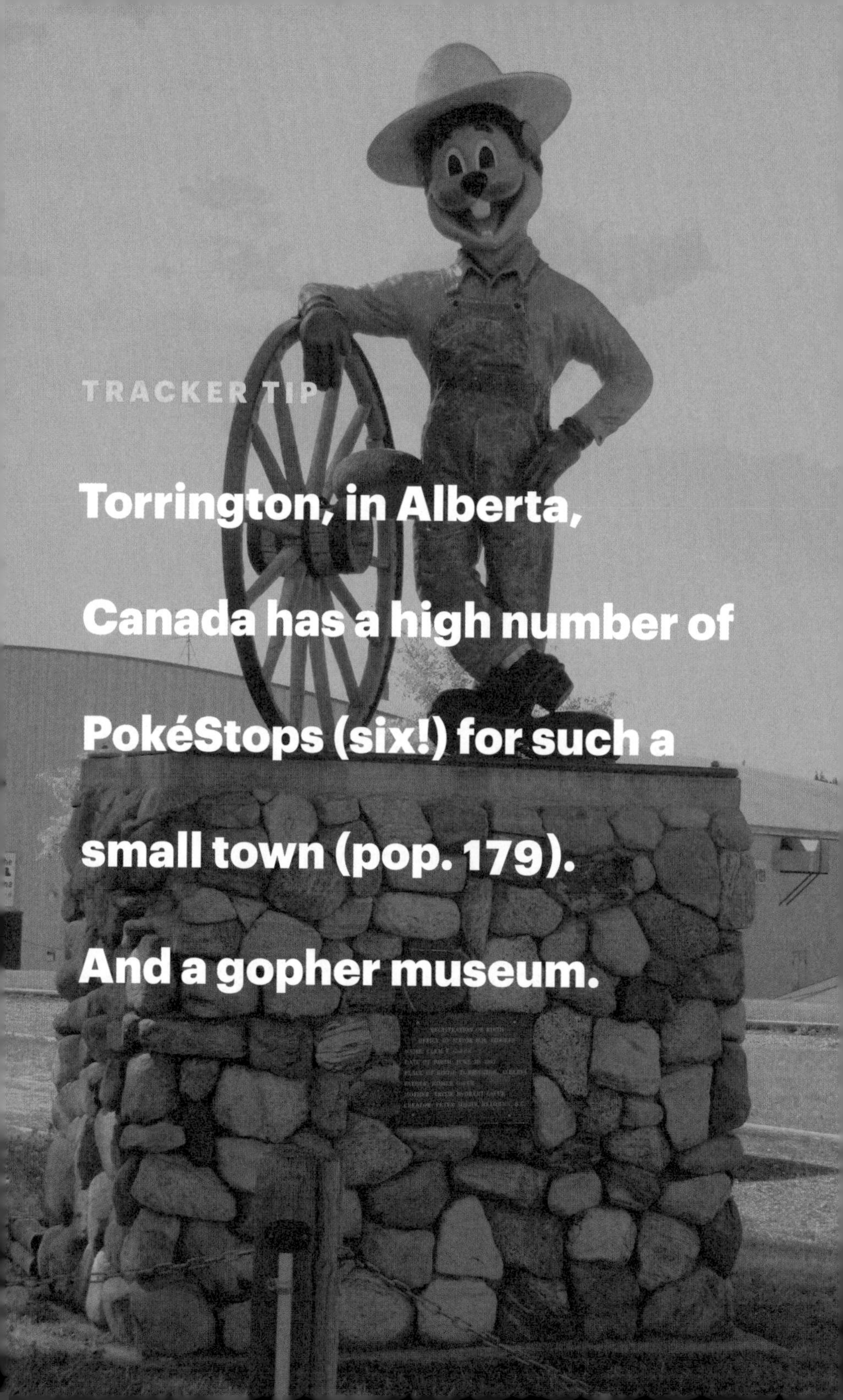

Torrington, in Alberta,

Canada has a high number of

PokéStops (six!) for such a

small town (pop. 179).

And a gopher museum.

large number of other people, catching Pokémon," Kira told the CBC. "It's fantastic to see so many people out and interacting and…just smiling at random strangers."

Torrington, Alberta, Canada

Gophers pop up throughout the prairies like Digletts, their little heads poking up and looking around. The cute creatures have earned their own museum in the town of Torrington, Alberta. You can visit the Gopher Hole Museum, which features taxidermied gophers thematically dressed and posed in dioramas.

The small town of 179 people has an absurdly high number of PokéStops (six!) for such a rural location, and the locals agree. Barbra-Lyn Schaeffer lives in the town and is getting tired of PoGo players. "We moved out here to be in the quiet, not to have people climb up over my fence. The last thing we need is strangers trying to peer in our windows. On Saturday, someone flew a drone up into our yard to play the game," she said. In fact, she's gotten so sick of disrespectful trainers that she's joined a class action lawsuit to get Niantic to settle with people who feel that PokéStop and gym locations infringe upon their privacy.

Bulbasaurs are hard to catch in the wild grass, according to the anime series. Given their difficult capture rate on The Silph Road, the show is correct. To make great catches, bring a lot of Poké Balls with you.

Be an Animal Lover
Tracker Tips

- **In Houston, Texas, two players came across abandoned hamsters** and alerted the local PoGo community. They never found the owners, but did get them to SPCA for help. The hamsters were named in honor of the game: Zapdos, Articuno, Mew, and Raichu.

- Trainers, when you're out and about catching Pokémon, be on the **lookout for other animals** that can use your help. When in doubt about what to do, please call your local wildlife center.

- Phylo(mon) is a Pokémon card game clone about **collecting real animals**. Find it at phylogame.org.

- Volunteer with your local birding society. Help them track bird counts while you're tracking Pokémon.

DANGEROUS AND OFF-LIMITS PLACES

One of the main reasons for Pokémon Go's appeal is exploration of cool places, and this book celebrates that. That being said, there are places one ought to tread carefully. You don't want to be on the news because you broke the law or, worse, got fatally wounded. Overly ambitious players do get mentioned and shamed publicly for irresponsible behavior.

Some of these areas are truly dangerous, and you can easily end up wounded if you're not careful. Follow the local laws and safety precautions so you don't end up joining a gang or losing a limb. Others are inappropriate places to play any kind of game, including PoGo. The last few locations in this chapter have requested removal from Pokémon Go because of the inconveniences and damage the players could or have caused.

Minefields, Bosnia

When PoGo launches, there's that warning to be aware of your surroundings, and that's a message that shouldn't be ignored—particularly when you're playing near minefields. In the 1990s, war in the Balkans devastated the countryside

and cost numerous lives. Some unstable mines still remain buried in the ground. The danger of landmine areas has prompted governments and NGOs, including Hungarian officials and Bosnia Without Landmines, to issue reminders that PoGo "does not take into account the minefields, so please pay special attention to signs." While playing PoGo in the country, you will find PokéStops dedicated to the tragic violence. One such PokéStop is Pali za slobodu, or "Fallen for Freedom" in English.

LOOK UP
Be extra careful when striving for the Kindler and Rocker medals.

This landmine warning exists in South Asia, too. The American government warned PoGo players to "beware of landmines or anything that looks like an old bomb" in the Vietnam region.

ONLY A TINY SLIVER OF SOUTH KOREA HAS ACCESS TO POKÉMON GO—AND NO ONE IN NORTH KOREA DOES.

North Korea and South Korea

On the Korean peninsula, two countries have effectively banned Pokémon Go for different reasons. South Korea has banned the use of certain mapping technologies out of security concerns, meaning that Niantic had to geoblock the nation. In North Korea, the entire civilian population is isolated from the Internet (tourists and authorized individuals can use it), and most North Koreans don't earn nearly enough to be able to afford a smartphone. Even if you were able to get around these obstacles, playing the game in North Korea would be dangerous due to the oppressive regime there.

On the southern side of the Demilitarized Zone between North and South Korea is the city of Sokcho, where all the PoGo players in the area are flocking. Due to a strange glitch in the way maps are banned, a tiny sliver of the country has access to the game. Sokcho Mayor Lee Byung-seon, who has proudly caught a Machop, loves that people are heading to his city. Some trainers have even taken to calling the

IN COQUITLAM,

BRITISH COLUMBIA,

THERE'S A POKÉ

GYM LOCATED AT

THE LOCAL HELLS

ANGELS CLUBHOUSE.

city Pallet Town. The city is rich with Pokémon, one player tweeted. "I heard Pokémon Go works in Sokcho, so I downloaded it, and caught eleven Pokémon just in my room." Sokcho is the farthest north you should go on the peninsula. Don't cause an international incident by entering the heavily guarded Demilitarized Zone!

Hells Angels Clubhouses

In **Coquitlam, British Columbia, Canada,** you can find a gym that is located right at the meeting place for the Hells Angels in the area. A spokesperson for British Columbia's anti-gang agency told the *Vancouver Sun*, "We think it's highly inappropriate that this game would include a location that attracts all ages—including children—to the location of

It's unwise to play in some dangerous places. In military bases, it's illegal.

a gang that is not only as well-known as the Hells Angels, but includes people who are involved in the highest levels of organized crime, including violent crime." It's best if you keep your battling to the gym and not with the individuals inside—even if you have a Machamp.

Similarly, in **Whanganui, New Zealand**, a Hells Angels pad was labeled as a PokéStop. When dealing with Team Rocket or Hells Angels, never go in on your own. One player visiting the stop knocked on the door and was told succinctly by a Hells Angels member, "Go talk to the police."

> When dealing with Team Rocket or Hells Angels, never go in on your own.

Military Bases and War Zones

It's unwise to go to some dangerous places. For others, it's *illegal*. Military bases and security agencies fall in this second category. Naval Air Station Whiting Field spokesperson Jay Cope made clear why this policy is necessary. "We understand the fun of the game; however, the integrity of the base and the safety of

IN INDONESISA, A FRENCH MAN WAS ARRESTED FOR PLAYING POKÉMON GO ON A MILITARY BASE.

its personnel are our top priorities," he said. In Indonesia, a French man was arrested for playing on a base.

Intelligence buildings are also off the list of places you should try. The **Pentagon** has blocked players from battling at the gym located there, while the Department of Defence has prohibited all employees from playing the game with government-supplied phones. **Vietnam**'s government has done the same, stating that PoGo shouldn't be played "near or inside the areas of offices of the Communist Party, the state, the military, and national defence sites and other restricted areas."

In a few years, we might look back on this serious military reaction to PoGo with some laughter. In 1999, the National Security Agency banned Furbies from their Fort Meade base. For now we can laugh at some incidents, like when Pikachu spawned during target practice, leading the US Marine Corps to tweet, "Get off the firing line, Pikachu! That's a safety violation!"

Although the **Israeli Defence Force** has banned its soldiers from playing the game, citing concerns around photos, location, and other information leaking, at least one American soldier has discovered the benefits of Pokémon Go. Louis Park made a splash tweeting an image of himself catching his starter, a Squirtle, in the middle of the **Iraqi desert** (he also challenged Daesh to a Pokémon battle). It turns out that much like the geography, the spawning locations of the Iraqi desert are ... empty. "On the front line, I was only able to catch the starters, but here in **Dohuk** they've got gyms and Pokéstops and everything," he reported. The game has helped relieve the boredom from serving in such a barren land, and he hopes that tweeting about his experiences will raise awareness back home of the troops' battle against Daesh.

Sewer Systems

The underworld is often underappreciated. Our civilization would collapse if it wasn't for the slimy, gooey, and especially stinky world of sewers. You probably don't think of these pipes carrying refuse from our toilets as noteworthy infrastructure—but we assure you they are. Without sewers, it would stink everywhere. It would be like a torrent of Grimers and Muks roiling through the streets. Gross!

Most of you wouldn't want to visit sewers because of the stench. But if you think catching a rare Pokémon is worth holding your nose, consider the injuries you could suffer if you fell into a tank. Concern for trespassing players caused the wastewater treatment plant in **King County, Washington,** to release a statement: "You and your friends could get seriously hurt and reduce your human hit points if you venture into one of our facilities. You know that terrible feeling you get when you accidentally drop your phone in the toilet? Imagine if you fell into a wastewater tank!... You certainly won't come out smelling like perfume, and you might catch more than Dragonite or Mewtwo."

Instead, be like Jason Englerth, who discovered some trapped ducklings under a sewer grate and got help to rescue them. While playing Pokémon Go on the streets of **Rochester, New York,** with his friend Josh Arpon, Jason heard

the ducks and acted by calling the fire department. He told the media, "I heard the baby ducks in the sewer drain, so I went and checked it out— and then I flagged down an officer and he got everyone out here." That day, zero Pokémon were captured,

Sometimes catching a rare Pokémon is not worth the risk. Consider the injuries you could suffer if you fell into a sewer tank. You certainly won't come out smelling like perfume.

but eight ducklings were freed and taken to a nearby wild-life rehabilitation center.

Like Jason, you can keep a look out for issues on your streets. The simple act of walking around hunting for Poké-mon can open your eyes to things that usually go unnoticed. Don't forget to look up from your screen while walking, though.

Transit Hazards

Looking at a screen while moving, whether on foot, by rail, or by car, presents many opportunities for serious injury. Don't do what Mark Correia did and *walk* on the Toronto subway tracks to catch Pokémon. The Toronto Transit Commission asks trainers to not do this, stating clearly that "it's an incredibly dangerous stunt that could have led to serious injury, or worse, or at the very minimum disrupted thousands of people's commutes." In an ironic twist, Corriea wasn't catching Pokémon while walking on the tracks; he was trying to make a satirical video to poke fun at the extreme lengths some players go to. The TTC announced that Corriea was fined $425 for unauthorized access to subway tracks.

Don't wear out your battery playing PoGo in case you need to call for a rescue.

In **Vancouver, British Columbia, Canada,** the popular local PokéStop and gym spots are all centered around SkyTrain stations. After an irresponsible trainer went on the track, the Vancouver Transit Police tweeted out important reminders to players: "Hey #PokemonGo players, we know you gotta catch 'em all, but stay behind that yellow line when on Skytrain," and "No virtual monster is worth risking your life."

If you're determined to be on a local train catching Pokémon, then head to **Düsseldorf, Germany,** where they have

the Pokémon Train. Rheinbahn runs the three-hour journey on their existing light rail network through the city with a strategy to lure players. The train travels at Niantic's walking speed to allow players to hatch eggs while passengers visit PokéStops en route.

As many trainers have learned the hard way, it's also unsafe to play the game while driving. One trainer in **Melbourne, Australia**, ended up crashing into an empty classroom at St. Francis Xavier College. The police were called to the scene and the player was charged with careless driving. "The nineteen-year-old did not level up or collect any stardust or candies, only debris from the crash," Victoria police spokeswoman Julie-Anne Newman told the *Age*. "Any Poké Balls, eggs, or potions the driver may have had remaining only attracted police."

HEADING TO

GERMANY TO

CATCH POKÉMON?

TAKE

DÜSSELDORF'S

POKÉMON TRAIN.

RESPECT LOCAL CUSTOMS, HISTORY, AND LAWS WHEN EXPLORING NEW AREAS.

Auschwitz, Poland

At one of the most infamous locations of the last century, Auschwitz, a museum spokesperson told the *Washington Post* that "playing the game is not appropriate in the museum, which is a memorial to the victims of Nazism." It should go without saying that playing a game in a place that is focused on remembering the Holocaust is not a good idea. Still, some people tweeted and posted on Instagram that they caught Pokémon there. The same thing happened at the Holocaust Museum in Washington, DC, and at the Foundation Memorial to the Murdered Jews of Europe.

Hiroshima, Japan

There are other locations where the game shouldn't be played. Hiroshima, one of two Japanese cities devastated by the detonation of atomic bombs during World War II, has asked that all PokéStops and gyms be removed from Hiroshima Peace Memorial Park. The inhabitants don't feel that it's appropriate to have Gastly and the like showing up, given the tragedy that occurred here.

Tuol Sleng Genocide Museum ·
Phnom Penh, Cambodia

The Tuol Sleng Genocide Museum has also put up signs asking trainers to play elsewhere. The museum is a memorial to people who were tortured, executed, or died of starvation in Cambodia under the 1975–79 Khmer Rouge regime. "Tuol Sleng Genocide Museum is not a shopping mall or a playground to catch Pokémon," one researcher said.

We don't think people who are defacing and disrupting these sites by playing the game are worthy of being called trainers, let alone Pokémon Masters. When deciding whether you should play in a place of cultural significance, use your best judgment and always err on the side of caution.

Bressolles, France

In France, there is a village of eight hundred people where you cannot play PoGo thanks to the mayor. Mayor Fabrice Beauvois mailed a decree to Niantic demanding that his village be delisted from the game. He argues that PoGo distracts people, putting pedestrians and drivers at risk in the town. He also worries that groups may gather after dark to play the game. In his words, the game has laid an "anarchical settlement" on the town.

Smart trainers know that you don't need to be right on top of a PokéStop or gym to activate it.

"When a cafe or a restaurant owner wants to open a business in any French town, they have an obligation to request prior authorization [from] the mayor. The rule applies to all people wishing to set up an activity or occupy a space on a public property. So it applies to Niantic, as well, even though their settlement is virtual," Beauvois told the Associated

Press. It's the first town to demand that the entire town be stripped of PokéStops, gyms, and even spawning points.

Private Property
Smart trainers know that you don't need to be right on top of a PokéStop or gym to activate it. Sometimes you can wait for random GPS fluctuations to get your avatar close enough. This means that there's little reason to break into private areas to play the game, though that hasn't stopped some players.

TWO PLAYERS BROKE INTO THE TOLEDO ZOO TO CATCH POKÉMON—INSTEAD, THE POLICE CAUGHT THEM

Around 2:30 one morning, two players in their mid-twenties, Robin Bartholomy and Adrian Crawford, decided to break into the **Toledo Zoo** to catch Pokémon. Instead, the police caught them. That's not much of a surprise considering that Bartholomy gave them advance warning on Facebook: "I am not above breaking and entering for a Pokémon." When asked about the incident, a police officer told the media, "The fact that you're playing a video game on your phone is not going to play well as an excuse in court." Let this be a reminder that you shouldn't break the law while playing PoGo.

Meanwhile, in **New Jersey,** another private property issue has arisen. A lawsuit has been launched against Niantic because a community's "once-quiet street degenerated into a nightmare." It turns out players were playing in a park after operating hours and making too much noise.

Gorilla Gorilla

TRAVELING TRAINER TIPS

What better way to play Pokémon Go than by seeing the world at the same time? The game's scope and player population of over forty million trainers are the features that make Pokémon Go unique and so much fun to play.

This guide encourages you to travel farther afield than you already do, and we want you to have a good time while you do so. Here are simple tips for making your travel experience better and more fun for other trainers you meet along the way.

Tips for Traveling Trainers

ENJOY LIFE

Be friendly to your fellow trainers and citizens. There is no reason to lose your temper or get mad at the game—as it's just a game, after all. Smile and be courteous to those around you. Try to be in the moment.

ENJOY THE VIEW

For good views, turn ON the augmented-reality camera in the game. We want you to enjoy the view while you're at the many beautiful or unique locations we recommend. Seize

the opportunities for fun photos of, say, an Exeggutor on the beach or a Lickitung tasting the backside of a statue.

TAKE YOUR TIME

Pokémon spawn several times throughout the day, so, in order to hunt all the Pokémon in an area, your best bet is to return at different times. When out tracking Pokémon, stop and smell the flowers or look around and take a moment to reflect on how PoGo has encouraged you to explore a new place. Be like Slowpoke and take your time to enjoy who you're with and what's around you.

USE YOUR POWERS

If you're going out for multiple hours, bring your charging cable for your smartphone. Better yet, bring a powered battery pack. If you have extra juice in your portable battery,

You don't need the Pokémon Go Plus to enjoy and play the game. These tips are for players on any technology the game runs on!

share it with other trainers. To have seemingly endless power, you can grab a solar-powered charger.

SAVE YOUR DATA

Despite what you may think, PoGo is generally an efficient application when it comes to your data plan. Unless you're part of the lucky elite who have unlimited data plans, though, you will inevitably want to use Wi-Fi to decrease your bill. Japanese Olympian Kōhei Uchimura learned this the hard way when he racked up a $5,000 bill playing PoGo

during the Rio Olympics. Luckily for him, his carrier retroactively charged him only for the unlimited plan.

BE ALERT AT ALL TIMES

No matter how tempting it is, *do not drive while playing PoGo.*

Please walk safely and be aware of your surroundings. Running is too risky if you're not watching where you're going, so check your phone only when you're taking a break.

Also, be cautious when it comes to your physical safety and that of your belongings. There's no need to go into dangerous neighborhoods or take other risks just to catch Pokémon.

During the first month of PoGo's release, many stories emerged of criminals using lures on PokéStops to attract players to locations where they would be vulnerable. Players would show up hoping for Pokémon and get mugged instead. After one such incident in Missouri, the local police noted that the criminals used the app to locate people who

Watch your data use: Japanese Olympian Kōhei Uchimura racked up a $5,000 bill playing PoGo during the Rio Olympics.

SEARCH FACEBOOK

FOR A LOCAL

PLAYING GROUP,

AND MEET NEW

PEOPLE BY

PLAYING POGO.

were congregating in a parking lot. These incidents seem to be rare, but trainers should always remember: safety first.

CHECK THE WEB

There are a lot of websites dedicated to PoGo and you should check them out for new information on the game. The Silph Road is a great resource and the community does some really neat data analysis. For Pokémon communities, you can search Facebook for a local playing group near you. Why not meet new people by playing PoGo and exploring a new part of the world?

CONSIDER THIRD-PARTY TOOLS

Niantic is firm on keeping third-party apps and websites out of their systems. They argue that third-party tools ruin the game experience. In the early months of PoGo, the third parties responded by claiming that

IN RURAL AREAS WITH FEW POKÉSTOPS, IT'S IMPORTANT TO SAVE YOUR POKÉ BALLS.

Niantic wasn't doing a good enough job for the players. No matter where you stand on the debate, these tools exist and you may be tempted to use them.

We don't have a stance on this debate, as it is up to every trainer to do what they think is best. We do have one warning: Niantic bans cheaters! Some third-party tools count as cheating, so think before using them. If you have been banned and you think it's a mistake, you can appeal on Niantic's website. Use unofficial guides, incuding this one, at your own risk.

Tips for Rural Areas

Rural players know that going too far away from urban areas makes for a more difficult hunt. You can make the long journey between PokéStops, gyms, and wherever else you end up much easier using these simple tips.

If you are new to the game, pick your team carefully, as you want to be with whichever one is dominant in your area.

It will help out in the later stages of the game because of how you get rewarded at gyms.

Plan your route in advance. There are third-party tools that can help with this process, or you can go out and explore on your own. Look for areas that have PokéStops and gyms close together to make the most of your time. If you know areas where your cell reception will drop out, avoid them, since the game requires an uninterrupted connection.

In rural areas with few PokéStops, it's important to save your Poké Balls. Justin Andress at Inverse provides this pro tip: "You can pick your Poké Balls up off the ground if you miss on your first go-round. It's a good way to keep your supply up."

While traveling between locations, remember that you can use incense to draw out Pokémon that don't show up on the sightings screen. If you do this, travel on side streets since the faster you go, the less area you can scan. Because the refresh rate on the map is fairly slow, you'll be driving

over areas that the scanner doesn't scan if you take faster routes. It may feel like you're checking more, but you're not.

If you want to live life on the edge, try the theme-song challenge. Play the theme song from the Pokémon challenge on repeat until somebody in the car catches a Pokémon. See who goes crazy first.

Tips for Urban Areas

Cities are filled with PokéStops, gyms, and trainers. The game is clearly designed to be played in areas with high density—so urban players are in luck.

We have seen Pokémon-themed bar crawls, tours, and other ways to explore cities. Keep an eye out for these, or plan one yourself!

Every city has one or more great locations with multiple PokéStops in one place with a gym. These areas are ideal places to meet other friendly trainers and get help playing

Don't forget to keep yourself powered, too! Bring a snack and water on your journey.

TRAVELING TO PLAY POKÉMON GO? MAKE SURE YOUR DATA PLAN COVERS THE AREAS YOU'LL BE EXPLORING.

the game. You can wander around and find the spot on your own, or you can search the Internet. Find online meetups that are announced on Reddit, Facebook, or elsewhere.

Remember to take precautions of general safety when exploring cities, such as not flashing your valuables willy-nilly like a silly. Don't play in the middle of busy streets or bike lanes. Be conscious of where you are.

Tips for International Travel

We have included a lot of international sites in this guide and we hope you visit them! This means preparing for international travel.

You will obviously want to make the normal preparations, such as booking your flights, grabbing your passport, getting a visa if needed, and acquiring the local currency.

To be a cosmopolitan trainer you need to do all that and more. Ash had to learn along the way and meet friends to help him get from city to city. But you can prepare for some

inevitable issues beforehand. Of course, we like to be like Ash and make friends along the way. During our research we have met many a character!

For international PoGo travel, make sure your phone works internationally and get a data plan for the areas you'll be exploring. Without the right data plan, you will only be able to play using Wi-Fi connections, which can be unreliable or difficult to find.

During busy seasons, you will want to book ahead to get the best hotels. We have stayed in hotels that have no PokéStops and hotels that have two PokéStops and three gyms. If you need to find out which hotel is the most efficient for your journey, ask local Pokémon groups or use an online PokéStop map.

TRACKER TIP
Here are some other
tips to keep in mind:
• Wear comfortable shoes.
• Pack a picnic.
• Catch only Pokémon,
  leave only lures.

For fun, consider gathering your own kind of gym medals from your travels. They can be little souvenirs to remind you of your Pokémon journey.

Tips for Respectful Travel

Every Pokémon trainer should respect the places they visit. *Respect* can mean many things depending on the PokéStop you're at. In some places you should be quiet, in some you should make a special effort to be understanding of cultural practices, and in other places you just need to stay out of the way. Being respectful means being aware of where you are and what was happening there before PoGo was released.

With too many gaming cultures, trash is an issue. Players regularly post messages on local PoGo Facebook groups about picking up garbage. The players encouraging people to clean up after themselves might sound like your mother,

but they're right: it's your responsibility to help keep Poké-Stops clean and enjoyable for everyone.

One Redditor, greenwomanoftheriver, wants players to take this approach of cleanliness and make it godliness. "Pokémon Masters could also become clean-earth warriors! Every time I take a walk, I take a plastic bag to put street trash in. It would be cool if more people did that. It takes no effort and gives the good feels."

People leave physical trash around PokéStops, and sometimes they also leave visual trash. In Washington, DC, some vandals spray-painted "Team Mystic" on a historical plaque. It's fortunate that Perry Edon and his friend live there

because they cleaned up the vandalism. They posted that all the teams came together to help them: "We cleaned it up. Mystic and Valor and Instinct came together to clean up an attack by Team Rocket." PoGo is a great game because it gets people to learn about the local community in a new way. All those historical plaques that are PokéStops are also showing people what happened there long ago. No other game has had such a large impact on local history as PoGo has!

It's great to see players learning about these areas, but it has led to some places being deemed inappropriate for players. Infamously, a player reported that they could catch Gastly in Auschwitz. A spokesperson asked Niantic to remove the PokéStops and stop Pokémon from spawning there, as it "offends the memory of victims." Such requests are common, as many sacrosanct locations exist all over the world.

Good trainers respect the people, practices, and places they visit.

If you go to a historically or culturally significant place, be sure to stop and take some time to appreciate it. No matter how tempting it is to catch the next Pokémon or level up faster in the game, you ought to put the game down for a few minutes and respect where you are.

If you do find a space that you think shouldn't be a Poké-Stop for cultural or other reasons, you can tell Niantic, via a form on their website. They do respond and are constantly updating their list of PokéStops around the world.

World travelers get to wake up to a new place and a new adventure every day. But only in the twenty-first century are travelers able to tap into the global Pokémon Go experience while satisfying their wanderlust.

Image credits

Adam M. Clare is author of *Escape the Game: How to Make Puzzle and Escape Rooms.* He is also lead game designer at Wero Creative, co-founder of Board Game Jam, and a professor of game design at George Brown College in Toronto, Canada. You can follow his research and find his games at RealityIsaGame.com.

About Page Two Books

PAGE TWO BOOKS is a publishing program that looks to the future. We imagine and create books that stay ahead of emerging trends and take a unique look at popular subjects. We commission original work from writers, designers, illustrators, and other creative people to publish books that fill clear niches in the book market. We are passionate about quality and original thinking.

www.pagetwobooks.com

**PAGE
TWO**
BOOKS